Traveling Mercy

poems by

Jennifer Bartell

Finishing Line Press
Georgetown, Kentucky

Traveling Mercy

Copyright © 2023 by Jennifer Bartell
ISBN 979-8-88838-404-6 First Edition
All rights reserved under International and Pan-American Copyright Conventions. No part of this book may be reproduced in any manner whatsoever without written permission from the publisher, except in the case of brief quotations embodied in critical articles and reviews.

Publisher: Leah Huete de Maines
Editor: Christen Kincaid
Cover Art: Andile Bokweni
Author Photo: Lester Antwan Boykin
Cover Design: Elizabeth Maines McCleavy

Order online: www.finishinglinepress.com
also available on amazon.com

Author inquiries and mail orders:
Finishing Line Press
P. O. Box 1626
Georgetown, Kentucky 40324
U. S. A.

Table of Contents

I. Departures

Traveling Mercy 1

A Re-Minder 3

Insomnia 4

When you write your mother's obituary, ... 5

Mercy 8

Mudskipper 10

Thread 11

Time is Everything 12

Flowers for the Living 15

Seashells 16

Her Who Peopled We 17

Scaling 18

The Road to Being Born 19

II. Arrivals

Insomnia 23

Woman of Steel 24

Survivor Call & Response 25

The Moon & Me 26

What Marriage Is 27

Fried Chicken-Neck Dinner 29

Dear Mikey, ... 30

The Setting Up 31

My Father's Shakespeare 33

S'posin 35

Leaves Like Prayer 36

L.J.'s Last Will & Testament 37

Lynches River, A Legacy 38
How to Die at a Wedding 39
What Marriage Is 40
White Shoulders 43

III. Returns

Insomnia 47
The Road to Being Born 48
the poet is thirty 49
Alice & Bessie 50
Ars Poetica 51
Taking Flight 53
Green Thumbs Elegy 55
Dear Ma & Da, ... 56
The Okra 57

Notes 58
Acknowledgements 60

In Memory of

Barbara McCray Bartell
&
L.J. Bartell

I. Departures

Traveling Mercy

In Memory of Goldie Graham, Blanche Lewis, & Genethea Eaddy

The Bluefield Griots plucked
me out of a jar before last breath
of prayer, buried me before birth:

This is how I time travel. I be seed
kept and passed, finger to palm,
planted and preserved for generations.

Recorded in the hulls are the movements,
the mournings, the joys. I listen
to the three Griots on the recording,

their one voice. These women-folk
with six bluing eyes that project
the gateway I need to bend

the arc of time. I wade through the low
tide of my own memory,
oysters fat and sure.

We arrive in Bluefield, buying
land to build a house.

Ma is crying in the outhouse.
No. *She is praying.*

Imagine the things you can tell
God with urine in your nostrils.

We step over Jim Crow to claim
our corner of America. Memories
perfect like they just came out the womb.

I loved with them in old refusing-to-fall
houses *where it rains on the inside*
while *hogs root around beneath the floor,*

snouts covered in mud. In the beginning
there was woods and the woods was good.
I *hunt huckleberries* and help haul

buckets of the dark fruit for tarts and jars.
I am heirloom seed: I remember the steps
of their lives, the joy of *iced tea so cold,*

your teeth would hurt; hands happy on cheeks
trying to hold the cold; this joy even
in their mama's smile and dresses stitched

together with cotton bract-scratched hands.
Before Bluefield was built up good
the Griots *planted corn, tomatoes, and okra*

on this land paid for with put-together money
stacked neatly in a sack. They didn't use all
the seeds. They put some of them in a Mason jar

on the shelf, waiting for the day to plant me,
to bury me down deep and good for new life.
The grave licks its lips, ready to swallow me.

I walk into the tide of memory instead, and
this is how my time traveling begins
as the Jonah-woman: My heart and mind

tucked in a place that can't be touched.
Me a seed in she hair and Carolina bound,
a seed that didn't crack on that ride in the hell-ship.

I a okra seed in she hair. Kept and passed,
finger to palm, plucked out of the jar before
last breath buried in the prayer of soil.

When fully grown, my yellow flower stretches
into green okra. Points its crooked finger to the sky.

A Re-Minder

Your best rebellion is breath's relay through your body.
Your best hope is with me in the infinite future.
You, "Johnson slave:" master's possession like the Johnson
mule, the Johnson house. Your names in wills:
Davey & Martha, Ben & Lena, Zula & Phil, Muldro & Minder.
Your name on my tongue is life after breath. You eat
out in the stables with the mare and consider the riddle
of chicken feet: Eat and pick your teeth at the same time.
My words are shards of broken dishes on your graves, breaking
the chain like Minder: a reminder of what came before.
I intercede for you across these rippled pages,
where you do not yet exist. I navigate Lynches River
between back thens and tomorrows, gathering you all
on my ferry boat. Tomorrow you will be at my table
with choice pieces of fried chicken, the baton in my pocket.

Insomnia

I sit on my front porch and I moan at the moon, its craters always remembering. The amaryllis leaves: limp and tangled, hug close to the porch. In spring it blooms, then sheds its red petals, clenches its hand into a fist it cannot keep, and crumbles on its own weight. A house built for five sleeps. A house built for five holds one in its hand, in the hollow of its stony hand. A house built for five can tell you stories that a house built for one cannot. A mosquito sips from my river, and I grant her a mouthful, only to swat her into my skin; broken wings linger on my palm. I look down the lane at the past.

When you write your mother's obituary,

she will be sitting next to you. Her face
unflinched in death's redundant river.
You will carefully write the scripture she
wants as her battle cry. You will write your
own name among the list of survivors.

When you write your mother's obituary,
she will tell you to record her funeral
arrangements:
>*No pink; only purple*
flowers. Do not spend too much money
on flowers; bury me in St. Mark, not
Jerusalem; don't bury me in them woods;
don't put no picture on my obituary—
I don't want to be face down in some
ditch somewhere; have them sing "I'll
Fly Away" when they wheel me out.

You will try not to think too hard
about what you are doing right now.
Later, you will carefully type these
last wishes and save them among
your poems. You will title it "Ma's Obit."

The next day you will go to work
and sit in a County Council meeting
for the newspaper you work for. "Ma's
Obit" is a seedling in your chest.
Sometimes it is hard to breathe,
so you go to a psychiatrist and

on the first visit, she makes you cry,
says it's not normal to work and go home
and nothing else. She tells you the story
of her father dying of cancer, but you
don't care about her father.

On the second visit, she says you may
need to get on antidepressants,
but you do not believe in them:
even if the pill makes you feel better,
it can't change the cancer eating
your mother's colon, liver, and lungs—
eating
eating
and eating
though it is already full.

Fuck her.

You stop going. You may have a friend
in Jesus, but you're not talking to him
right now. The now sapling in your chest
is getting too much water and light.

You still get up and go to work
until your mother quits chemo
and you take a few days off so your father
can have a break from stiff-arming death.

When you watch your mother take
her last breath, it will be raining, your father
will be crying and you will feel your mother's
hand snap several branches off the sapling,
but its roots will be intact. She will flashback
to the moment she held you in her arms
for the first time.

When the funeral home director comes
in his shark skin suit, he will give you a paper
outlining the obituary and order of service.
You will open the document "Ma's Obit."
You will copy and paste it into a fresh
document, you will pick the last
dress she will ever wear, you will pick
pearl earrings.

When you write your mother's obituary,
you write your past obituary.
You are the twin oak in the backyard
standing and observing, shedding
leaves and acorns.

Mercy

As I pray for Ma to die, I meditate on your merciful love.
Your name is supposed to mean mercy.

Every story I know about the Bible I learned from her, Sunday
School teacher at Matthew Hill Holiness, where she

went to school, where her father played the drums, where her Ma
was one of The Mothers of the Church in the Amen Corner.

I know the story of the woman with an issue of blood. How she
touched your hem and was instantly healed. I know there is power

in your name, dear Jesus. I know that death is a healing, not a punishment,
or a curse, but how all life ends. But, why cancer?

Why let it spread instead of your mercy or your capacity to work miracles?
What kind of savior are you if you refuse to save? My prayers are not enough.

I can see her reaching for your hem, her hand a dodgeball,
you leaping. Jesus leapt. And I wept into the bible of my clasped hands.

There were these long spells of time when we had tranquility,
days when I wouldn't utter a word to you, days I stayed out with Ma

because she didn't want to catch any germs at church. Ain't that ironic?
She didn't want to go to church to get sick, to keep her white blood

cell count up, to avoid the issue of blood so her body would be strong
enough to take the chemo. But now I am begging you, this my only prayer:

Save my mother's life by taking it. I cannot lie down to sleep
listening to her catch her breath, oxygen machine bubbling

like an aquarium. This song of my mother trying to breathe on repeat.
Her breath like a lullaby and a nightmare, my love for her strong

and weak in this unknown. I don't even know if you are
listening anymore, but if you can't make her whole again,

please just take her now. If your love is merciful. If your mercy is love.

Mudskipper

Deep waters
and I cannot swim or float,
so I sink like a stone.
Why I never learned to swim?
Why did my mother not teach me?

My Ma is fifty-eight years old
when her mother's ninety-five-year-old hands
tried to rub the pain away. Hands that had no
power. *I knewed I wasn't going to see her again,*
granny would later say.

Ma left the world without knowledge
of navigating the waters of living
without a mother. Her toes never wet
in its throes, no lick of water touching
the tight curls on the top of her head
as she sits on the banks in a one piece
watching me sink: *I've given you all
you'll ever need in this world.*

I am a stone at the bottom of a woman-built
lake, a stone who grew gills and learned to live
in the deep dark bottom I built for myself.

Until I grew fins and swam back up
to the water's surface, gulping for air,
destined to be one who walks on land.

The beauty mark above her lip, that beauty mark
that was like a period at the end of a sentence,
smiled at me: *That's it. That's my girl.*

Thread

The smell of her finds me
when I am
looking for a needle
in an old brown and black purse
she used as a sewing bag:

My tears sprinkle on her skin.
The hospice house is quiet.
Tropical Storm Ernesto dumps
rain on us. My father cries
Don't leave me, Bobbie!
Bobbie, don't leave me!
      but she has already left.

We wait for the funeral home.
I lie down in the hospital bed
and rub the back of her hands.
Her jaundiced eyes do not close,

even when I put my hand
over them like they do
in the movies.
    Still.
I try to close her eyes
because I don't want her to
see what comes next.
She may be dead, but she's not
blind. She still smells like her living self.

The funeral home is here.
I watch them zip
her up in the black bag.

Time is Everything

i. 2006
Her legacy to me is
polyps in the colon.

Ma say, *Roasting a turkey
in a bag is for people
who can't cook.*

*The more time you have,
the more flavor you will have.
Time is everything.*

We saved the wishbone
year after year, hung it over
the doorframe for luck.

How old was she
when her first
polyp began its slow brine?

ii. 1953
For Christmas we always had
apples, oranges from Flordy.
And always de niggertoes
from Brazil.

(Dey called dem niggernuts
too. De toes or nuts: soft
parts that hung and easy
ta slice off.)

Our Ma Moonsie put
the nuts in her cakes.

Folks walked for miles
ta visit one another
back den. Moonsie

baked for dem. And dere
was no freezer,
only a small ice box.

Moonsie wrapped
de cake in wax paper
and towels
and put de cake
under de bed.

We was so poor,
our main meal was
grits and beans.
I mean grits and beans
for breakfast, lunch,
and dinner.

But we always had
cake for company.

How clean up under de bed
musta been. To be de place
a cake went to rest while waiting for
company to come in and shake
the dust offa dey shoes.

iii. 2014
Saturday is clean-up day.
Always keep the house clean.
You never know who's going
to stop by, Ma say
when we were little.

I still do. Keep
the house clean.

I read Ms. Lucille. She brings
me tiny packages of light:
such letting go is love,

I let go the lesson of the quiet house

I let go cobwebs in the corner
I let go the dust on the clock
I let go the schedule of the four o'clocks
I let go the clutter in Da's barn
I let go the *lesson of the falling leaves*

But I do not let go
of the memories that stand
on demand at the end of the hallway.

Nobody is coming to this house
and I sit with that for hours.

I walk into the kitchen for my recipe
book, where I hand wrote some of Ma's
original recipes. I'm cooking company
chicken tonight. It's smothered chicken
so good that company could eat it.

I let go the wishbone.
Luck is not in the bones or the blood.

Flowers for the Living

Ma melted
        metaphors
in her cast-iron skillet:
        Give me my flowers
while I'm living.
        I can't enjoy no
flowers when I'm dead.
        It was spring,
the sun was shining.
        I was a little
girl who wept
        when the dog died.
I went to the vacant
        lot next door
to pick daffodils.
        I bunched them:
Five yellow
        heads poking
from brown hands.
        The black beauty
mark above
        her lip smiled at me.
She placed the daffodils
        in a vase of water,
until their heads fell,
        looking down
at the blue tablecloth.

Seashells

My mother's salty vomit
can't find solace. She's rough
and bumpy, though
sometimes smooth. I am
but a comma in her belly.
She is sometimes found
whole, or in pieces. I find
her on the seashore, her hard
outer layer, her soft
insides somewhere
in the ocean. She is brown
in my dreams, other times
she is a translucent, slick
with all colors of the rainbow,
tumbles out of the salty ocean.
I find her on the shore,
squinting, waiting for her soul
to wash itself.

Her Who Peopled We

I a swampwater
Geechee looking
out 'cross this ocean.
Every shore of the Atlantic
a reminder of death and birth
of shells, skulls, hulls
broken slave ships
and her who tied and toted
my line with her
'cross these waters.

Her looked up
between the slats of wood.
Saw the shining moon
from the belly of the ship,
The everlasting moon
I gaze at tonight.

Her one of me:
Eaten
but not swallowed.
Her a oblation,
who went through the Door of No Return
but came back with me.
Her always comes back
for me, even when I leave myself.

Her comes back.

Scaling

> *She would rather be the one deciding what she keeps*
> *and what she throws away.*
> —Nikky Finney

The river shimmers; its color mirrors
my own. I search for bream, spots,
bass, croaker, and shad. They bite
good today, the last bit of water
evaporates from their lungs, blacks their eyes.

Tiny round translucent rainbows
fleck up into the sky as I scale
the first fish, cut it open: clean
the insides out, leave its head on.
Saving the shad's eggs
for *Ms. Everlina's Country Caviar:*
Boil fish roe. Pour water off. Cool. Peel 'em.
Put 'em in oil. Stir it round. Put a lid on it.
Beat 3 or 4 hen eggs with salt and pepper
in a bowl. Pour in with roe. Fry the hen
eggs with the fish eggs.
Serve with grits.
The sturgeon
has nothing on this delicacy.

Ma rests. The surgeon
scaled her cankerous colon,
cleaned her insides out.
I save the tumors for biopsy
stew I will eat later.

Waiting in and out of water,
in hot oil and closed rooms.

The Road to Being Born

is a long one, treading much trouble. Black
tea-stained river water pours into the eager mouth
of Winyah Bay where it intertwines like a braid
on its way to the Atlantic.

On this road we pass haunted tobacco warehouses
in Hemingway: the auctioneer's voice,
waiting for fall to make him flesh
again with the scent of sweet cured tobacco.

To cross into this world, I cross many water
worlds, with woods in between.
Tall pines line both sides of the road,
as if they are lights lining a landing,

waiting for my descent.
I am ready to step into myself and enter
this realm, the height of it all
pulsing hard in my blood.

I slip through the slit in my mother's belly,
the smell of marsh water
in my nose. My parents only prepared boy
names, but I am Abena, her who comes

on Tuesday. On the road home we go
through Muddy Creek. The soft rush of water
like the lullaby of my mother's blood:
Choppee, Peter and Deep Creeks.

At Granny Moonsie's white house in the middle
of a tobacco field, she stares down at me and mourns
the arrival of another girl-child who may drop her books
and then her panties for any man. We pass

the building where men in white hoods strategized
where to burn the next cross,
which was a piece of the road down
from the old Huggins Place where Ma was born.

And then finally home. Home in the quiet
blue of the field, the quiet chaos that is the
swirl of voices whispering to me in tongues
I will only remember when I go back

down the road, when I cross over
into the other blue and slip under the slit
of the horizon to start this pilgrimage again.

II. Arrivals

Insomnia

The ghost did not float. I jolt awake. Stare into blackness. Particles of flashbacks in the atmosphere. It's so dark back here. I rise into the night. The stars welcome me. Road: a panoramic view of what will never be again, a familiar stranger who saw: broken noses and baseball bats, the one room house where cracked-out Cuda-P once dwelled, basketball courts made of black dust. These images danced around me that night; I could not dance back. Forgive me. Jack Daniels helped craft this plot. When the old people died, the love left. What is lost goes underground, blossoms as a seed-choking root. Love left when the old people died. We want them back. Forgive us.

Woman of Steel

In Memory of Everlina Jacobs

Everlina: The Woman of Steel,
stitched together with barbed
wire and broken bone.

Raised up her husband's chilren
and mammied some white chilren.

But when she tried to carry her own,
they *got stuck in her stomach.*

I listen to her speak about seeds
that grew deep in her body, seeds
she couldn't pluck into the cradle
of her arms. The Lord has a way
of having his way.

Imagine seeds in her black
earth. Unable to hear the bright sun
and heavy rain of her voice.

The doctors *whipped* her *ovaries back.*

Her hips girded
with barbed wire never birthing,
frozen in time, cold and empty
like my own womb.

Everlina is nobody's mammy.
Everlina: Woman of Steel,
everybody and nobody's mama.

My bright river of full moon
appears on my panties this month.

My womb still full of nothing
but blood   again.

Survivor Call & Response

In Memory of Alice Ann Eaddy & Bessie Chandler

Alice Ann	Bessie
I told them I don't have no cancer	It was frightening
spot in the lungs in 2011	lump in the breast in '96
chemo and radiation	chemo and radiation
remove it with laser radiation	in case one little cell got away
coming back on the lower lung	lump, lymph nodes removed
I believe in the Lord	Lord, it's in your hands
don't worry about it	and that took the fear away
the worry will get you down and sick	don't let the fear of it get you down
some people let it burden them	have a positive attitude
down: don't do that	don't let fear get in there
I thank the Lord that I am a survivor	it won't let you survive

The Moon & Me

You are so big and naked.
Your light pours down on me
and in this gaze is grace.

A gauze of clouds cannot hide
you and this thin cloak of words
falters in the face of your beauty.

You make me moan when I want
to laugh. You, oh great timekeeper,
are the same moon of mother

and father and their mothers and fathers.
You determine how the waters flow,
how the blood runs. On your white

pockmarked face I see a mirror
with craters: the gaping holes
in my history, the hallowed, ravaged

origins of me razed
by slavery. You show me
myself and nothing.

What Marriage Is

You stand in the kitchen
with your black steel-toe
boots. In front of you
is a platter of fried
chicken.

Your mouth is easily
greased with the words
maid and slave that you place
at her feet,
a gift men give women.

You would have her yield,
but she would not let
her neck be wrung
with your words.

This is how I learn
the term *male chauvinist pig*:
It falls out of my mother's
mouth like a shield.

Kitchen table lessons:
food and fickle follies
of men, who kiss
and dis with the same mouth.

You never knew about that house
Ma and me
secretly planned to flee to,
and we never knew your daddy.

How he grieved over his dead
child, how the meanness seeped
out of him each time he sipped
too much white lightning.

You were once me watching
this scene. You too committed
it to memory. You always loved
the chicken neck best.

Fried Chicken-Neck Dinner

Skinny, yet
    elegant,
    scant
on meat,
    golden crispy
    brown.
He fixes
    broken things.
    Grease and grit
of the day
    washed away
    from his stout
fingers.
    Done
    piddling
in the barn.
    Thighs and breast
    reserved for
him.
    He picks
    the neck.
Grips it
    with two hands,
    snaps
the delicate
    vertebrae,
    broken
in his mouth.
    Meat sucked off:
    polished neck
bones
    rest next
    to white rice.

Dear Mikey,

Long-suffering is a synonym for patience,
and is an ancestor of prison.
You are freezing all the time.
Your cellmate talking all day and all night
ain't good either. You feel like your mind
'bout gone, like his. I'll call the warden
about it tomorrow.

I warn you: yesterday
is the only honey in my mouth.

Is it weird around the house without Da?
you want to know. Not weird,
just empty like the inside
of my beating heart. Sometimes
the pendulum in his clock swings,
but mostly it does not. I always say
hello when it does.

When I finish writing this, you will
still be in prison and our parents
will still be dead. The daytime moon
will be with us all day. We waiting
for the day we don't have to write
your name with six numbers behind it.
When we can call you by the name
Ma and Da gave you.

All of the bricks, all of the barbed
wire between us is nothing like
the circle of silence that wraps
around me when I sit under
that pendulum, with time beating above
my head. Did you know your name
means *Who is like God?*

Patience is long-suffering. The next time
you ask me how things are going, I will say, *Michael.*

The Setting Up

They cook a big pot of pileau,
fry fish, eat pound cake from Piggly Wiggly,
drink store brand soda
and hear auntie complain about it:
How you gon bring some sto' brand soda?
Nobody wanna drink that mess.
They cook catfish stew and bring
barbeque from Scott's.

This is the setting up.

I look at the funeral wreath on the door,
glare into the funeral light on the front lawn,
the house overflowing with people,
mud on the kitchen floor, plastic
cups everywhere.
Take shots of Crown with my brother
Maine. Mikey still locked up.

All these people, this food, this drink, can't fill
the place where my father once was.
All these people, all this food and folks setting up
with me.

I am so tired. So tired.
I just want it to be over:
The people laughing and talking
over my grief like it's a ghost already.
But it ain't ghost, it still got flesh yet

and all this does is set me up in a false hope
of comfort; they will disappear
like last time when Ma died. Grief will move in,
live with me for two years;
she'll put herself in my pocket and walk
with me in the grocery store. She'll be hovering
over my bed when I try to sleep.

All this good food will be gone,
all of these well-meaning
folks too, but Grief,
that wily gal,
won't go nowhere.
And she won't even have a plate of rice
with her to share.

My Father's Shakespeare

He was a man of few words. Not a *How
art thou?* kind of guy, but would greet

with a *Hello, my Amerikees!*
This Shakespeare book sits

in his barn as if it were born here.
An old portrait of Jesus hangs

from a beam, a fishnet
just above it; Shakespeare is just under our Lord.

This Shakespeare is not mine.

How many days would he sit in the door
with Shakespeare and parse the words?

*After the body comes, where it goes is
of no consequence.* And maybe this book

is of no consequence too.
Did he carry it as he plowed the garden?

I can imagine him saying, *Look here, Billy: I reckon
we can make this work.* I see him draw a crooked

line between Shakespeare and the King James
Bible. He dropped out of high school

and returned in time for integration,
but he had already had his education.

He brought me papers to examine after Ma died. I read
to my father, but all the while he had his own readings he kept

to himself, like his brother J.C.'s obituary
he kept tucked in his truck's glove compartment.

The silence between us is like the water
between Charleston and Lagos. I could never

hear him. There are many chasms in my studies
of my father. So much he has taught me

in his death, so much life in the silences.

S'posin

S'posin I got to my father's grave
and harshly raked across it
all of my resentful gratitude.
Shucks, my Pa wasn't nothing
but a country boy who loved
his sow-belly slightly burnt.
Independent, and full of agony,
he could talk any fish outta
the river and onto his hook.

S'posin my daddy wasn't dead
and I walk into the house as
he is shelling field peas he
coaxed outta the ground his
own self, even though it's winter
and the frost falls softly on the ghost
of the collard greens.

S'posin I used my grief to pave
the inside of my heart. And it
stopped, like his, doing this thing
we love, our hearts aching for who
we can never have again. Our smiles
cowering openly, searching for a way
to escape all that is coming.

Leaves Like Prayer

This is what leaves like a prayer:
the collard greens my father planted.

A collard is a cabbage that does not develop a heart.

Their green leaves are like hands
about to clasp in solemn devotion,
arching towards the sun for a blessing.

My father sleeps in his grave.

And the collard greens he planted
keep growing in his autumn garden.
The frost sweetens them
and the time comes to reap what dead
hands have sown. My brother cuts
the green hands from the earth's body.
the green prayers do not leave the black earth.

But here we are. At the table with turkey
and stuffing. Clasping our hands over
his greens drenched in hamhock juice.

We eat prayers.

This we do in remembrance of him.
Take. Eat. His love
grown for you and me.

L.J.'s Last Will & Testament

Use the money to settle bills.
Except that bill from the triple-bypass.
They gets nothing.
My heart gave out in the middle of my barn
when I was getting tools to fix a sink.
No. We won't pay them nothing.

Estate tax, income tax, then more taxes?
When will they be done with me?
The money wasn't mine to start with no way.
They're done with me.

To my three children all I own.
Half the policy between
the eldest and the youngest,
middle child likely
in the jailyard or graveyard.

Eldest child born last is my personal representative.

Signed in my careful and slow hand.
My people ain never had nothing.
I am the son of sharecroppers.
I came into this world alone.

Lynches River, A Legacy

My father wears patience
on his brow as the boat
slices through the blue
mirror of the black water.
Our hands dig into a can
of dirt. The worm twists
and contorts, is threaded
onto a hook, dangles
like an ornament.
My fingers grasp for crickets,
the prick of their jagged legs,
brush of antennas, quick.
I cannot capture the crickets
like I capture these moments
of the last time I went fishing
with my father. I see the fish
gulping air near the surface.
They winnow the worm
to nothing, careful
to not get caught on the hook.
My father wears patience
on his brow in the way
his father taught him.
As a little boy he coaxed
the fish. Kissing them
onto the hook. Puckering his
lips like fish do when they
try to find water but only
gulp the drowning air.
My nephew is eight
holds the bass by its mouth,
coaxes the patience in his blood.

How to Die at a Wedding

Do it slowly, not on purpose.
Gaze at the wedding colors:
burnt orange, brown foliage.
A moment of silence for
the bride's dead father
is your moment to slip back in time:

See your father from years ago.
How he held your hand,
never got a chance to walk you
down the aisle, except at your
Ma's funeral. Look up at the bridal
arc and kneeler and see a coffin
laden with purple and white flowers.

Live in that coffin, breathe in
that coffin with your dead Ma
for a few minutes. Hear the rain
pattering on the roof while
the two of you lie there.

Your Ma turns to you and says,
The rain means I made it to the other side.
You know you have to go back now.

And so you do. The moment
of silence for the bride's dead
father is over, but you feel
like you're breathing underwater,
broken seeds in your clenched fists.

What Marriage Is

> "My beloved put his hand by the latch of the door, and my heart yearned for him."
> —Song of Solomon 5:4

i.
He learns to change her colostomy bag,
how to clean it, how to keep
the stoma pristine.
His acts deep,
deep like whatever flows
beneath the Black River.

Love baptizes a man. He can hold
his wife's shit in his hands.

ii.
He stands over himself, his earthly dwelling
thrown off. Confusion settles low on his brow
stalling his next step,
he smells her coming to the barn door.

Let's go, L.J., she whispers.

iii.
Lights flash
on the dark road to the hospital.
He woke me up at 4 a.m. and said,
Your mommy can't breathe.

The red lights
are the only stars on this dark road,
sirens silenced. Ma in the back
on oxygen.

Ma cannot breathe.
I cannot lose her.
I cannot breathe.

~

Blue lights flash
off of his white
T-shirt as he speaks to the officer
who was hunting for my brother.

My old lady's sick, I hear him say,
oxygen warning sign on the back door.
I have never heard him call her *his old
lady*. He says it with love and sorrow.

iv.
Ma stands at the barn door,
grief sloughed off like second skin.
Her body beckons endings
of mourning. She enshrouds her gown
around him, the him who had stepped
outside of himself, and carried
him beyond the ceiling of sky.

v.
This is their story before I am born,
before they knew they had so many stories
that would outrun their blood:
I am the right hand of my mother swearing
obedience in the Kingstree Courthouse.
Back when they were Negroes, down the road
from Black River, the King's Tree, now ash.

vi.
He catches his breath
and stares at her; he does not see
her nose caked with blood,
or flesh sagging off her
bones, or her hair shorn
with the sword of chemo.
He sees her
on the day he married

her: shining black hair,
beauty mark winking,
her smile showing her gapped
teeth, which he had always found
beautiful.

His hair had come back too.
Trading his silver beard
for black, strong running back legs
underneath him.

Bobbie, don't leave me again, he whispers.

This isn't heaven.

It's something better.

vii.
This is my parents
after they are dead,
after they know the many stories
outliving their blood,
whispering the words down
to me through a tiny hole in the sky.

Love is stronger than death.

If this love be strong,
if this love be faithful,
let me rest my hope on such
love, that I can have it for a time.
That I can have a man not afraid
to take my shit.

White Shoulders

A plume of cigarette smoke hovered
over the corn stalks as he palmed

the cobs, shrugged at the thought
of White Shoulders, the perfume she

wore, the bottle he kept in his pocket.
When they were apart, he kept her

with him. The scent of her was as close
as the smell of dirt and dust after plowing

when the wind carried traces of it and triggered
his days working in Tarheel tobacco fields.

Fresh earth-wounds open to accept a seedling
that will never sprout, stays buried until

the trumpet waters it to life. At goodbye
he could smell her brown skin still,

even through the purple-ladened coffin.
He smelled it even when he drove past

a fire-curing tobacco barn in mid-August.
In a wave that rushed his barn door,

he smelled her again. She came to get him.
And in his pocket: a receipt for Dr. Pepper.

III. Returns

Insomnia

I look down the lane at the past and see him looking up at the stars. Stars like crack rocks tonight. He wishes he could scoop them up, place a price tag on each. I look up. The vast sky holds so much light and still is so black. I watch and keep silence as the logs in the burn barrel crack in the night. I can see his breath, but he can't see me. I am still at some unknown point in the future. Once, farmers auctioned cured tobacco; they sell directly to Big Tobacco now. Some other leaf is being auctioned, under the thin veil of the stars. As day breaks, I see a mangy white girl walking up and down the road.

The Road to Being Born

He wasn't the one holding the baby's heart
in the center of his body. He wasn't
soaked with the sacred sweat
of laboring with the stubborn
one they named Michael.

Something about a woman's parted
legs makes a man hungry: fried
chicken, coleslaw, mashed potatoes.

On return the doctors say they must
cut his second son out of the womb,
she wanted tubes tied, he did not:
The decisions we make when
we are full.

On the road back to Bluefield, Ma
is silent, sizzling, her path to motherhood
still gurgling like all these
rivers and creeks they cross to get home,

and three years later,

when they come back down
that road with me nestled
under her rib, they are sure:
I am only daughter, born last.

the poet is thirty

after Lucille Clifton

I have such knowledges as
                                        snakes have
the smell of water
                the sound of grief
where the cracks are
                            I am comfortable
hugging the door
                I quiver over myself
in the darkness
                                and I will leave loneliness
when I can

Alice & Bessie

In Memory of Alice Ann Eaddy & Bessie Chandler

Say what you must
about the strong Black
woman—melanin superpowered,
cheating time with their smooth faces.

But let's say a word here for these two:
Alice & Bessie: The Alphabet Women,
Ain't your Mammy or yo' Auntie.
Alice & Bessie: Alpha & Beta:
Warriors fully girded
with the whole armor of God.

They will say they are strong,
not knowing that when you're weak
is when you're strong, and though the delicate
frozen multiplication of cells holds its breath,
it eventually exhales to an unthawing: Cells
spread like dandelions in the wind
finding any slit of concrete to squeeze into
and grow and grow and grow and grown
full on the sidewalk, which by now is full
of dandelions who gently blow away
one by one by one by one.

Ars Poetica

Let others that know more speak as they know
—Wordsworth

Girl child
jumping ditches, sweat-kissed
with azalea nectar.

I know then what I know now:
I am the poet
in the throat of the bird
on her lonely flight,
fleeing the chaos at dawn,
sheltering the girl sitting
inside of herself,
inside of the house.

Standing
out in the distance, I wait for my
selves to come back,
wait for the bird to call me home,
to call the home in me out.

My first poem stands out
in the distance. Pausing
and cooing like the first
bird perched on the tree
of forbidden fruit. Pecking
at the flint flesh of knowledge
until she broke seed.
Sweat-kissed with the poem
that had been trying to escape
me before I was born.

My first poem stretches out
of the palm of my hand
into lives long past and lives longing
to go so they can come back.

Reclaiming every bit
of word stored up.

I am ghost and ghost maker,
I do not speak truth,
only what I know to be true:
I am the fisherman's daughter
with net and oar.
I am the poet
in the mouth of the fish.
I am the seamstress's daughter
with my needle and thread.
I am the design
in her pattern.

I come with much work
and the light ain't long.

Taking Flight

> *To die is to return*
> *To fly is a bird's heart.*
> *Neither is freedom.*
> —Chris Abani

When the storm is over,
they are back on the broken
branch of a tree, singing.
The storms didn't break
their wings or their voices,
but that doesn't mean
they weren't scared,
that their little hearts
didn't almost beat out
of their little chests.

I watch the hummingbird
from my window,
how she fights other
hummingbirds.
Flying is a way of freeing,
a way of fleeing.
Fighting for survival,
running everyone away.

To be a hummingbird
dipping my beak
into the sweet of life!
Beating my wings
furiously,
a small thing made
of feathers, struggling
for balance,
trying not to be swallowed
whole by the sky.
Beating my little wings,
and trying to live

even when the world
says I should die,
deserve to die.
Beating my little wings,
beating even the sky,
beating my little wings
to the sweet of life.

Green Thumbs Elegy

Plastic poinsettias
are dusty on their graves
not as red as the roses
growing in the front
yard in Bluefield.

Ma planted flowers,
Da planted vegetables.
Their green thumbs gray
under the weight of the grave.

Plastic poinsettias
have never been seeds
and don't know
that to be born,
you must first die,

to be alive is to live
like a daffodil
during Eastertide.

Dear Ma & Da,

At night, a few stars dot a blotted-out sky. I don't feel at home here,
but this is where I have made my home. I had to come up out them woods.
I'm too young to be this old. That girl sitting in the house, reading a book,
writing a poem, baking a cake, that lonely girl wasn't created when
you died. She was there before you eloped in a country courthouse,
before your sons were born, before the earth that makes Bluefield
had been formed. I thought I had left her behind in the house
in Bluefield. But she is with me everywhere I go. She is here. She came
up out of the woods with me, though I could not see her then. I
tote the memory of you with me and plant you deep in this field
                                              of words.

The Okra

My sacrifice will not
be in the pot with the field peas.
I will not find myself in the heat
of a cast iron skillet,
or breaded and bathed in oil.
Some of us will have new life
in a seafood gumbo. Others will
be chosen to live again.
I was grown to be reborn.
Brown, dry on the stalk, as if I
would die, looking
abandoned and clothed in purpose:
Seeds inside for next
generation's harvest.

NOTES

"Traveling Mercy" uses fragments from a 2012 joint interview of Bluefield residents and sisters Goldie Graham, Blanche Lewis, and Genethea Eaddy aka Ms. G. Also included in the interview was Ms. G's daughter Elizabeth Eaddy. They are all now deceased.

In 1963 Warren Barr sold the first parcel of an eleven-acre tract, formerly known as Poston Farm. Barr was a World War II veteran and farmer. The land is located three miles west of Johnsonville, South Carolina city limits. The tract and neighborhood would later be named Bluefield.

The poem "A Re-Minder" uses information from *As Time Goes By: Johnsonville and Surrounding Areas* by Rebecca Hughes Dunahoe. The city was known as Witherspoon's Ferry and Johnson's Ferry before becoming Johnsonville. The names that appear in this poem come from the wills of wealthy, slave-owning farmers who died during the 1800s in Johnsonville. Additionally, "Johnson's Ferry was the point from which the stagecoach driver stopped to change horses. As the stagecoach passed east over Lynches River on the ferry a Johnson slave in charge of the ferry mules announced the number of passengers with a blast from a fox horn—one blast for each passenger, thus informing Mrs. Sarah Johnson of the number of places she should set for dinner."

That Lynches River was named after Thomas Lynch, signer of the Declaration of Independence may be historically inaccurate. Plats pre-dating the signing of the Declaration show that the river was referred to as Lynches Creek.

In the poem "Mercy" the aquarium simile is borrowed from Ed Madden's poem "Reef," which appears in the chapbook *My Father's House* and the book *Ark*.

"Time is Everything" uses the words "niggertoes" and "niggernuts," which are colloquial nicknames for Brazilian nuts. Some lines in this poem are from Lucille Clifton's "the lesson of the falling leaves." Special thanks to Aunt Helen for providing her Christmas memories for this poem, which I use as my mother's memories.

The epigraph for "Scaling" comes from Nikky Finney's *Head Off & Split*.

The city of Georgetown, South Carolina is referenced in the poem "The Road to Being Born."

Da is pronounced like Dad but without the last "d." It is not pronounced duh/dah.

The poem "Woman of Steel" uses fragments from the 2012 interview of one of Bluefield's first residents, Everlina Jacobs, now deceased.

The poem "Survivor Call & Response" is entirely phrases from a 2012 interview of Bluefield residents Alice Ann Eaddy and Bessie Chandler. Both are now deceased. The poem "Alice & Bessie" is also based on them.

"After the body comes, where it goes is of no consequence" is a quote from a Shakespeare play.

"the poet is thirty" is after Lucille Clifton's "the poet is thirty two."

The epigraph for "Ars Poetica" comes from William Wordsworth's *Prelude.*

The epigraph for "Taking Flight" comes from Chris Abani's *Sanctificum.* The poem also makes a reference to Emily Dickinson's "Hope" is the thing with feathers.

ACKNOWLEDGEMENTS

Grateful acknowledgements are made to the editors of the following publications in which the following poems have appeared in slightly different form:

As/Us: A Space for Women of the World: "She Who Peopled We" & "Poemcoming" (appears as "Ars Poetica,")
Blackberry: a magazine: "White Shoulders"
Callaloo: "Traveling Mercy" (appears as "Three Muses of Bluefield") and "Leaving Chicago"
Composite{Arts Magazine}: "Insomnia" in Part I (published as "This Starry Night: Front Porch")
decomP: "Scaling"
The Double Dealer, Pirate's Alley Faulkner Society's: "Last Will & Testament of L.J." *Fall Lines: A Literary Convergence*: "Taste the Sound" & "Blue Edge" (fragments of both poems appear throughout the collection),
KAKALAK: "Re-Minder" (appears as "Minder")
Kinfolks: a journal of black expression, Kinfolks Quarterly: "My Father's Shakespeare" published as "Shakespeare in the Barn,"
Obsidian: Literature & Arts in the African Diaspora: "when you write your mother's obituary"
The Petigru Review: "Thread,"
pluck!: The Affrilachian Journal of Arts & Culture: "Mudskipper,"
The Raleigh Review: Literary & Arts Magazine: "Leaves Like Prayer"
Sense of the Midlands: "Lynches River, A Legacy" published as "Fishing with Dad"

Without Bluefield, I am nothing. Many thanks to the people of Bluefield, past, present, and future. You have all contributed to my development. Special thanks to my neighbors who allowed me to interview them in 2012/13 and are included in this collection. These women sat down with me and told me their stories; however, they did not live to see this publication: Bessie Mae Chandler, Alice Ann Eaddy, Golden Graham, Genethea Eaddy, Liz Eaddy, Blanche Lewis, Everlina Jacobs. I am forever grateful for their lives and their words. I hope that I honor their memories here.

Thank you to the following poets, writers, and organizations for their support and guidance during the writing and revision of poems in this collection: Candace Wiley and Monifa Lemons-Jackson, co-founders of The Watering

Hole Poetry Organization, thank you for creating a space for poets of color in the South. The poets who have facilitated at TWH Poetry Retreats I have attended and whose workshops and lectures have guided me during revisions: Lita Hooper, Remica Bingham-Risher, Tyehimba Jess, Frank X. Walker, Roger Bonair-Agard, Mariahdessa Ekere-Tallie, Darion McCloud, Jericho Brown, Tara Betts, Randall Horton, Ebony Noelle Golden, Dasan Ahanu, Evie Shockley, L. Lamar Wilson, Sharan Strange, and Bettina Judd. My professors at the University of South Carolina who read early versions of this book: Ed Madden, Sam Amadon, Scott Trafton, and the late Lynn Weber. The Callaloo Writing Workshop of 2014: Vievee Francis and Gregory Pardlo; I continue to take with me the lessons I learned from you both. The Furious Flower Poetry Center, especially Joanne Gabbin. To the poets, writers, professors, mentors, and friends I've had over the years who have been wells of encouragement along the way: Dianne Owens, Terrance Hayes, Emilie Duck, Melissa Dugan, Dustin Pearson, Willie Tolliver, Christen Cozzens, Rachel Trousdale, Chris Abani, Tracy K. Smith, Ching-In Chen, Maya Marshall, DaMaris Hill, and to anyone whose names I may have forgotten, charge it to the head and not the heart.

Special thanks to homegirl-sister-friend Nikky Finney for her careful line edits, guidance, and encouragement over the years.

To my family, all the Bartells, McCrays, Boykins, and Harvins, thank you. Special thanks to my brothers, Maine and Mikey. My late parents L.J. & Bobbie Ann: I'm forever blessed to be your daughter. To my husband, Lester Boykin, thank you for freeing me with your love and always having my back.

Jennifer Bartell is the Poet Laureate of the City of Columbia, SC. She grew up in Bluefield, a community of Johnsonville, SC. She received the MFA in Poetry from the University of South Carolina. Her poetry and nonfiction has been published in *Obsidian, Callaloo, pluck!, As/Us, The Raleigh Review, kinfolks: a journal of black expression, Jasper Magazine, the museum americana, Scalawag,* and *Kakalak*, among others. An alumna of Agnes Scott College, Jennifer has fellowships from The Teachers Guild, Callaloo, and The Watering Hole. She teaches at Spring Valley High School in Columbia, where she was named the 2019-2020 Teacher of the Year. She is pursuing a Master of Library and Information Science at UofSC to become a school librarian. You can reach her online at www.jenniferbartellpoet.com.

www.ingramcontent.com/pod-product-compliance
Lightning Source LLC
Chambersburg PA
CBHW022149180426
43200CB00028BA/466